SOCIAL RESILIENCE
A Primer for All

Enhance Social Experiences and Foster Social Resilience

AZHER HAMEED QAMAR

DEDICATION

This work is dedicated to the children caught in war, hunger, and fear. You are a ray of hope, a symbol of life, a beacon of love, and a vision of humanity.

SOCIAL RESILIENCE: A PRIMER FOR ALL

Introduction

ACKNOWLEDGMENTS

I extend my sincere appreciation to all those (social workers and migrants) who shared their experiences, perspectives, and insights with me about social integration and togetherness. I also acknowledge that cultural diversity is a resource that allows for a comprehensive exploration of social resilience.

INTRODUCTION

For the last three years, I studied the concept of social resilience within different frames of reference (such as social psychology, climate change, crisis, and migration studies). The more I delved into the characteristics of social resilience, the more I departed away from the non-social views on social resilience that restrict it to merely a psychological understanding of human resilience, excluding the socio-political and socio-ecological dimensions of human lives. I found social resilience a dynamic concept that is complex and embedded in human-environment interactions and contextual diversities. Also, the interdependence of human in the social world evolves and contributes to their transformative experiences with changing environments.

Social resilience is a relatively recent term that relates to the social dimension of resilience. Initially defined as the ability to respond and withstand (crisis), the concept of social resilience has evolved into a multidimensional fluid concept that addresses learning and adaptation in many different kinds of contexts. Human interdependence develops and contributes to our transitioning experiences in changing contexts. Ultimately, it is all about our lived experiences. Social resilience is shaped by our social experiences and interactions with the political, economic, cultural, and social environments. Hence, we need to recognize social resilience as a social phenomenon that, when fostered by better social experiences, may contribute to collective and holistic well-being.

In my study of social resilience in the context of

migrants' lived experiences and social integration, I defined it as a socially constructed process (to survive and thrive together) shaped by social experiences and practices in the face of environmental changes and challenges. If I were to define social resilience in simple phrases that everyone (including children) could comprehend, I would say that it is "the experience of surviving and thriving together".

In this short primer, I present a brief description of key characteristics that contribute to the process of social resilience. This primer is a pocket guide for everyone who wants to make a difference in collective social well-being. This primer provides powerful keywords that express the social aspects of resilience-building strategies, leading to better social experiences and greater social well-being. I hope that this social resilience primer will give a thorough understanding of how to promote social resilience through enhanced social experiences and behaviors.

The art of thriving together is not hard to master.

Azher Hameed Qamar
www.drazher.com

August 2024

Ground - Connect - Grow

A

ADAPTATION

Adaptation is a process that develops the ability to adapt to challenges by adjusting to changing environments. The power and success of adaptation depend on willingness, acceptance, flexibility, and readiness to cope with changing conditions in life. Adaptation connects us to our ever-changing living environment and helps us improve our social experiences. Throughout the process, we learn how to use and restructure our daily experiences for coping and transformation.

The comfort zone is a barrier to adaptation.
Evolve out of the box.

BONDING AND BRIDGING

Bonding takes place when we build and strengthen strong ties, usually in the form of families and friendships. Bridging allows us to extend our ties beyond family and friends. Bridging facilitates the formation of connections between in-groups and out-groups. Bonding and bridging are both crucial aspects of social capital, which is a valuable resource for social resilience. Bonding and bridging serve as the cornerstone for a fulfilling social life and overall well-being.

Interdependence is a social resource. Trust and reciprocity are the foundations of interdependence, contributing to a functional social life.

C

COLLABORATION

Collaboration is a process of engaging people, groups, and organizations to establish a shared understanding of problems, coordinated efforts to address problems, and a progressive commitment to achieve common goals. Effective collaboration, when integrated with joint initiatives, multiplies the ability to attain the highest level of shared goals. Collaboration is required for social expansion, effective networking, and constructive cooperation; all of these contribute to social resilience.

To increase effective collaboration, inspire yourself (and others) with clarity, integrity, and prosociality

D

DIVERSITY

Diversity is an important aspect of social experiences, particularly in multicultural societies. It is about reconciling differences with recognition, respect, and acceptance. Diversity enhances our ability to learn to live together while embracing differences. It is also a way to develop togetherness with social cohesion and empathy. Diversity allows us to learn from different perspectives and experiences, that can help us develop resilience strategies.

A salad bowl's nutritional value comes from its many different ingredients, which provide the best nutrition while preserving its unique taste and flavor.

E

ENGAGEMENT

Engagement on a social level refers to the act of interacting with others to provide and receive social support. Engagement promotes social experiences by involving individuals, groups, organizations, and institutions in a socially active system. It enables people to extend their social networks and advance their social connections, contributing to social well-being. People who actively engage themselves with their surroundings and social circles improve the quality of their social lives.

Be consistent in connecting with your social environment and take the initiative to develop meaningful relationships.

F

FACILITATION

Facilitation is the action of providing support to improve response to issues and challenges. We all have different abilities, and we are capable of doing some things but not everything. We must connect and integrate our skills, talents, and abilities to help each other to attain our full potential. Facilitation occurs during social encounters when people connect for various reasons. It is important to acknowledge that facilitation is a pro-social action that supports individuals and communities in developing a shared understanding of their needs and support.

Facilitation is a virtue that can be developed through unconditional prosocial practices.

G

GRATITUDE

Gratitude is an important step toward acknowledgment, generosity, and appreciation. Gratitude is the warmth of social experience that sets the basis for prosocial behavior and socially valued relationships. It is the practice of recognizing, appreciating, and utilizing what we have in our lives, such as people, things, and opportunities that help us to grow and develop.

Gratitude transforms our belongings into the strength to develop and grow over time.

H

HARMONY

Harmony is about connecting with us and those around us to build a pattern of social relationships that promotes collaboration for the sake of collective well-being. Harmony is achieved by mutual respect, understanding, tolerance, and acceptance of diversity. It is also about finding a balance between individual and collective needs for the greater good of the community.

Maintain harmony in social relationships by practicing 3R; Respect, Reciprocity, and Receptivity.

INCLUSIVE INTERACTIONS

Inclusivity refers to including everyone in all opportunities and resources. It is a fundamental human right based on the equality of all human beings. Inclusive interactions imply engaging with all people on all levels. It is about establishing and utilizing inclusive environments to obtain a rich experience of social interactions while embracing diversity as a means of strengthening connections and expanding support networks. Inclusive interactions promote knowledge and learning through social participation.

Differences should not be used to rank people. Differences should be utilized as a resource to bring people together in social interactions.

J

JOINT ACTION

Joint action is the coordination of two or more people/groups (or organizations) to effectively deal with challenging situations for shared goals. When people work together, their strength and potential multiply, enhancing their ability to survive under difficult circumstances. Interconnecting people as social actors is a key component of social resilience. Joint action facilitates a shared understanding of crisis and coordination in resilience-building strategies.

Experience the power of joint action and collaboration to achieve the best during the worst conditions.

K

KNOWLEDGE-SHARING

Knowledge encompasses both awareness and comprehension of information, facts, and social realities. Knowledge-sharing refers to the exchange of knowledge, learning, and skills that facilitate collaborative problem-solving approaches. Knowledge-sharing enhances both theoretical and practical understanding. Sharing knowledge fosters the process of resilience by providing access to a diverse range of skills and abilities.

Knowledge-sharing bridges the gap between the known and the unknown by encouraging contribution and the exchange of information.

L

LEADERSHIP

Leadership is the act and skill of leading and guiding others. In the context of social resilience, leadership consists of the capabilities to be aware of (self, others, and the environment), purposeful reflexivity (on change and challenges), taking initiative, and establishing a support network. Leadership develops over time by practicing and developing these capabilities.

Effective leadership prepares people for teamwork by improving their coordination in shared responsibilities that promote collective growth.

M

MANAGEMENT

Management is the process of dealing with situations using various forms of organization and control. By following management strategies, successful management ensures that the system continues to work. In difficult situations and circumstances, management also plays an important role in connecting people and resources to endure and recover from the crisis. On a social level, we may call it 'social management', which refers to the management of social institutions and organizations that deal with social coexistence and community engagement in social projects.

Effective management requires multi-tasking skills. It implies interacting and acting on multiple levels simultaneously.

NETWORKING

Networking, in the context of social resilience, refers to social interconnections such as family, community, and other social relationships. Networking serves a purpose in crisis management given that it allows people to share their sense of risk, responsibility, and care. Individuals and groups can use networking to integrate social and psychological resources and to carry out rehabilitation and intervention collaboratively.

Effective networking is NET – Nourishing, Empowering, and Transforming together through thick and thin.

O

OPTIMISM AND OPENNESS

Optimism is a psychological tool for gaining control of our nerves during a crisis. It is a psychological capital that connects hope, confidence, and efficacy to move forward. Optimism prepares us to face, and experience change while striving for the best. Openness is the quality of being open and considerate about new experiences with people and the environment. Optimism and openness work together to improve social resilience by embracing challenges and exploring new opportunities.

Optimism and openness optimize (enhance) and open (expose) the way to success by triggering inner strength and sense.

P

PARTICIPATION

Participation is the act of being actively involved in something. In the context of social resilience, it is a social activity that involves people in interactive collaborations to deal with challenges. Participation brings people together at various levels of mutual engagement to accomplish tasks together. This is also a resilience approach that promotes a sense of shared responsibility and coexistence.

Participation offers the opportunity to create an inclusive social space and support network where 'I' merged into 'we'.

Q

QUALITY

Quality is a powerful term that has a significant influence wherever it is used. As a noun, 'quality' is a standard for something. However, as a term having a positive impact, 'quality' suggests a level of excellence. In the social context, quality time and relationships play a key role in fostering social resilience. Quality time is meaningful time spent with devotion and commitment to accomplishing something or interacting with others in various contexts. Quality time spent together builds quality relationships, which contributes to increased social participation and stronger social networking.

Be qualitative - it is demanding but worth doing.

RECIPROCITY AND RELATIONSHIP

Reciprocity is a type of mutual exchange cooperation in which individuals or groups enhance their relationships by exchanging support in a variety of ways (such as resources, services, and skills). Reciprocity develops healthy and functional relationships by connecting people through trust, confidence, and selflessness. Reciprocity also increases the impact of resources and services through sharing and exchanging.

The sustainability of the whole ecological system is based on the philosophy of reciprocity, and so should the social system.

SOCIAL SUSTAINABILITY

Sustainability, though a normative term, is commonly defined as progress toward meeting current requirements and planning for the future. Sustainability's long-term goal is to coexist with our environment. Social sustainability is a human rights-based strategy for building inclusive and empowered societies in which the social and political systems promote diversity, equity, and well-being for present and future generations. Social sustainability is a constant process of understanding current and future human demands and connecting various environmental resources in society.

Understanding the human-nature interaction and applying this knowledge to collectively surviving and thriving can lead to social sustainability.

T

TRUST AND TOGETHERNESS

Trust is a sense of security and confidence that develops long-term and productive relationships. It is the foundation of friendship, love, relationships, and togetherness. Togetherness is a state of happiness that occurs when we feel close to and welcomed in a community. Togetherness is an experience of connectedness and empathetic relationships. Trust and togetherness encourage people to coexist, collaborate, survive, and thrive together. Trust has a reciprocal value in togetherness; hence, there is a shared sense of survival and growth, which promotes social resilience and wellness.

Here's a TIP for developing and enjoying togetherness: Trust (belief and confidence), Integrity (truth and honesty), and Parity (equality and justice).

U

UNITY

Unity is about working together as a whole, with each part helping to strengthen the collective power. In the context of social resilience, unity is associated with social cohesiveness, integration, and collaboration, as well as a belief in coexistence. In this sense, unity corresponds to various other aspects of social resilience, including togetherness, engagement, reciprocity, networking, collaboration, and bonding.

The strength of a rope required for making a boat is determined by the number of threads and the twists that bind them together.

V

VULNERABILITY AND VIGILANCE

Vulnerability is usually connected with the conditions that are exposed to risks and hazards caused by external factors. It is necessary to recognize and understand vulnerability through vigilance. Vigilance means being aware of changing circumstances and obstacles. While vigilance entails actively engaging with changing circumstances and events, it also aids in organizing the social movement for preparedness, planning, and implementation of resilience strategies. Vigilance promotes social resilience by raising awareness and enabling effective and timely responses to lessen vulnerability.

Recognizing vulnerability through proper vigilance is essential for our transitional and transforming experience in the face of change and challenges.

W

WILLINGNESS

Willingness is the deliberate intention to do what is required under certain circumstances. It is a state of being willing to join and contribute without being pushed or hesitant. Interestingly, willingness influences actions by connecting internal and external motivations. For example, a shared awareness of risk and responsibility can motivate people to collaborate and cooperate to achieve common goals. Hence, willingness is desirable to support actions that advance the process of social resilience.

Willingness is a will to live together, and this is a way to collective well-being.

X

XENODOCHY

Xenodochy is a term (used in the early 1700s) that described hospitality and courteous behavior toward strangers. A xenodochium was a facility in early medieval Rome where foreigners and strangers may be welcomed and helped. The term remains relevant to build support networking and a sense of coexistence, acceptance, tolerance, and cooperation in multicultural societies. In other words, xenodochy is a necessary social characteristic for cultivating selflessness while acknowledging diversity and inclusion for mutual growth and development.

Diversity is beautiful; tolerance is a virtue; and acceptance is an action that brings beauty and virtue together to build a progressive, inclusive society.

Y

YIELDING FLEXIBILITY

Flexibility is the ability to adapt to changing conditions. It enables us to cope with adversity. Yielding flexibility is a coping strategy that involves being open to change and challenges, as well as adapting and adjusting when required to navigate challenging situations. In connection with the social aspects of resilience, yielding flexibility is a characteristic of adaptive social behavior that promotes social competency for a collective understanding of risk, recovery, and growth.

Flexibility is a skill that we acquire and enhance as we interact with other people, perspectives, and situations.

Z

ZEAL
(enthusiasm for sociability)

Zeal is an intense word that describes passion and determination to achieve a goal. In its social context, zeal is an excitement for socialization that brings people and communities together. It advocates for a communal effort to shape their adaptive and transformative skills by helping one another through sociability and connectivity.

If you want to bring people together, simply take the initiative and show your enthusiasm through interactions and practices.

BRAINSTORMING

1. What is *adaptation*?
2. What qualities are needed for successful adaptation?
3. How does adaptation help us in our social experiences?
4. What is *bonding*?
5. What is *bridging*?
6. Why are bonding and bridging important?
7. What is *collaboration*?
8. Why is *diversity* important?
9. What is *engagement* in a social context?
10. How does *facilitation* help in social life?
11. What is *gratitude*?
12. How is *harmony* achieved?
13. What does *inclusivity* mean?
14. What is the purpose of *joint action*?
15. What is *knowledge-sharing*?

16. What is *leadership*?

17. What is *social management*?

18. What is the role of *networking* in social resilience?

19. How does *optimism* help in a crisis?

20. What is *participation*?

21. What does *quality* time mean in our social lives?

22. What is *reciprocity*?

23. How does reciprocity help in building relationships?

24. What is *social sustainability*?

25. What is *trust*?

26. How should we build trust in our social interactions?

27. What does *togetherness* mean?

28. How does *engagement* improve social well-being?

29. What is *vulnerability* connected with?

30. What does *vigilance* mean?

31. How does vigilance help during the crisis?

32. What is *willingness*?

33. How does willingness influence actions?

34. What does *flexibility* enable us to do?

35. What is the purpose of flexibility in social lives?

36. How can we practice social resilience to survive and thrive

SOCIAL RESILIENCE

KEYWORDS

Keywords used in this primer to enhance social experiences and foster social resilience.

acceptance	exchange	planning
acknowledgment	excitement	preparedness
adaptation	facilitation	prosociality
adjustment	flexibility	quality
appreciation	friendship	receptivity
awareness	generosity	reciprocity
balance	gratitude	recognition
belief	growth	recovery
belongingness	happiness	reflexivity
bonding	harmony	relationship
bridging	honesty	resource
clarity	hope	respect

coexistence
cohesion
cohesiveness
collaboration
commitment
competency
confidence
connectedness
connectivity
consistency

contribution
cooperation
coordination
determination
devotion
diversity
efficacy
empathy
empowering
engagement
enthusiasm
equality
equity

hospitality
implementation
inclusivity
initiatives
integration
integrity
interactions
interdependence
justice
knowledge

leadership
learning
love
management
motivation
networking
nourishing
openness
optimism
organization
parity
participation
passion

responsibility
security
selflessness
sharing
sociability
socialization
support
sustainability
teamwork
togetherness

tolerance
transformation
transition
trust
truth
understanding
unity
vigilance
vulnerability
well-being
willingness
xenodochy
zeal

MY

SOCIAL RESILIENCE

WORKBOOK

A - Adaptation

"Change Challenge" - Write or draw about a time they adapted to a new situation and how it helped you.

B - Bonding and Bridging

"Family and Friends Web" - Create a web of connections where you list family and friends and describe how each bond supports you.

C - Collaboration

"Group Project" – Write about an activity where you work together on a small project, like building a small model and what did you learn about teamwork.

D - Diversity

"Cultural Collage" - Create a collage that represents different cultures and what they can learn from each other.

E - Engagement

"Community Helpers" - List and write about people in the community who help others.

F - Facilitation

"Helping Hands" - Write ways you can help others and support each other in different situations.

G - Gratitude

"Gratitude Journal" - Write a note of thanks for the things you are grateful for and why.

H - Harmony

"Peace for All" - Write steps that we should take to cultivate peace and harmony around us.

I - Inclusive Interactions

"Inclusivity Bingo" – Play a bingo game and check off activities like playing with someone new or learning some words (such as greetings, thanks, welcome) in another language.

J - Joint Action

"Team Challenge" - Organize and report a team activity
(such as building a paper town) that requires working
together.

K - Knowledge-sharing

"Teach and Learn" — Write about what you can teach others (such as a game or a skill).

L - Leadership

"Leadership Role-Play" - Role-play different scenarios (such as treasure hunt game) where you practice being leader. Write how will you lead your group.

M - Management

"Organize It!" - Create a plan to organize a small event
or task (such as lunch together, classroom cleanup)

N - Networking

"Social Network Map" - Draw a map of your social connections, like family, friends, and community members.

O - Optimism and Openness

"The Good Box" - Write down positive thoughts and things you look forward to, or good memories that inspire you, and put them in a decorated box.

P - Participation

"Participation Journal" — Write a journal where you track your participation in different activities and reflect on your experiences.

Q - Quality

"Quality Time Journal" – Write a journal to document how did you spent quality time with family and friends.

R - Reciprocity and Relationship

"Reciprocity Ring" - Write about ways you give and receive support in different relationships (such as at home, school).

S - Social Sustainability

"Eco-Friendly Pledge" - Write pledges on how you can contribute to a sustainable future, like recycling or conserving water, or eco-friendly travelling.

T - Trust and Togetherness

"Trust Circle" — Write what trust means to you and how you build trust with others. What do you expect and what do you do for trust and togetherness.

U - Unity

"Unity Art" - Create a large poster (and paste its picture here) that represents unity and includes contributions from different children.

V - Vulnerability and Vigilance

"Safety Plan" - Create a safety plan for different scenarios, like what to do in an emergency.

W - Willingness

"A Wall of Willingness " – Post notes about things you are willing to do to help others, and how will you do it.

X - Xenodochy

"Welcome Cafe" – Write a concept about a 'Welcome Cafe' that welcomes new children and shows how you can make them feel included in this welcome cafe.

Y - Yielding Flexibility

"Flexibility Tree" - Create a tree where each leaf represents a way you can be flexible and adapt to changes.

Z - Zeal (enthusiasm for sociability)

"Zeal Book" – Recall your social experiences, and document your passions and what you were excited about in your social interactions.

www.drazher.com

Azher Hameed Qamar, an established scholar in the field of social and behavioral sciences, combines his experience as a qualitative researcher with a strong interest in understanding human lived experiences in social settings. Qamar investigates social resilience and social integration using qualitative research approaches. His research connects social experiences and practices, highlighting the significance of context and meaning in social interactions. To read more about his work, visit www.drazher.com.

Art of thriving together is not hard to master.